HARDPRESS.NET
HOME OF HARD-TO-FIND BOOKS

Soviet Russia
by Albert Rhys Williams

SOVIET RUSSIA AND SIBERIA

ALBERT RHYS WILLIAMS

Ten Cents

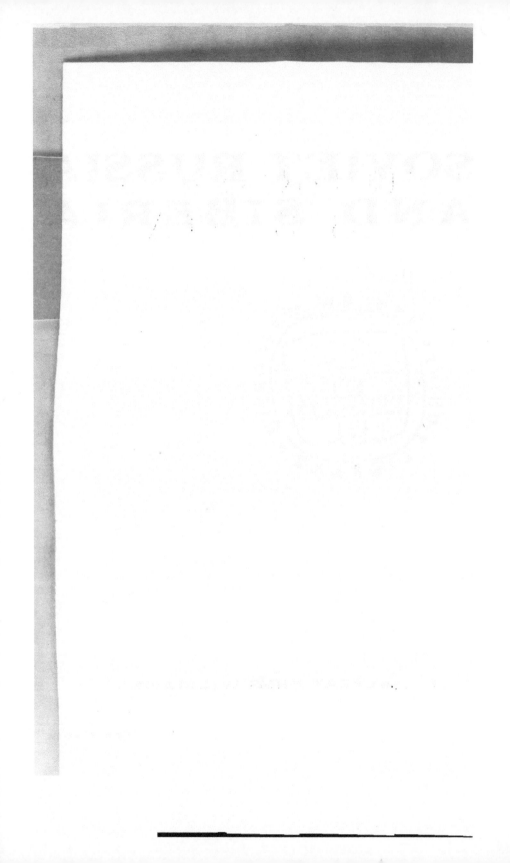

SOVIET RUSSIA
AND SIBERIA

BY
ALBERT RHYS WILLIAMS
From an Address at the Ashland Auditorium and
an Article in the New Republic

CHICAGO
CHARLES H. KERR AND COMPANY
CO-OPERATIVE

SOVIET RUSSIA AND SIBERIA

"To the last syllable of recorded time mankind will have cause to regret that the people of America and the people of Russia did not understand one another during the years 1917 and 1918." These are the words of a member of the Root mission to Russia.

Of course, being in Russia does not necessarily qualify one to understand the country if one lives isolated from the deep currents of the common life. Some one said of the Root mission that it knew as much about the habits, ideas, and customs of the Russian people as a submarine commander knows about the habits, ideas, and customs of a fish.

How Are Your Customs?

We get only little scraps and glimpses of the whole truth. One time I was in a little village near the Volga as the guest of Ivan Ivanoff and his wife, Dusa. We were gathered around the table celebrating a holiday.

I was remarking about the strange Russian customs and how different they were from American. "This great common bowl from which each man eats directly. (I generally managed to get my spoon in first.) That is a queer custom," I said. "Yes, I suppose it is," agreed old Ivan.

The chickens came in to pick up the crumbs from the floor. Something stepped upon my foot. I thought it was a dog, but I looked down into the upturned eyes of a pig. "Queer custom, this, to have pigs and chickens in your dining room," I commented. "Yes," nodded Ivan, "I suppose we are a queer people."

"And that big stove which takes up a third of the room, and the tiny little windows," I added.

Just then the baby in the mother's arms happened, in baby fashion, to lay its feet upon the table. The mother, very quietly, but looking straight across the table at me, said: "Here, baby, take your feet off the table. Remember you are not in America. What queer customs you have in America!" (Laughter.)

There is some truth in this statement that Americans put their feet upon the table. And there is some truth in all the exaggerao nitsand violent assertions made about Russia, but there is about as large a grain of truth in them as there is in the assertion that Americans as a rule put their feet upon the table.

"The truth about Russia," on which I am slated to talk, is a very large order, because Russia is a very large country and the Revolution is a very large affair.

The Five Per Cent Suffer

A revolution is like any other conflict. There are the losers and the winners. The losers in Russia represent less than five per cent of the population—the Black Hundred, officers, landlords, etc. With them, idealogically, goes another ten per cent of the people. All these are full of rancor and bitterness toward the Soviets. And for this they have reasons enough.

I am not so devoid of imagination as not to know the sufferings of all this upper class, suddenly shorn of its privileges and compelled to go to work, and the dismay of all those Russians who suddenly have been made to step down from the roof-garden. I am fully conscious of all the cruelties which are part of this class war which rages in Russia. But this has been told over and over again in America. In fact we have reflected here only the attitude of one class involved in the revolution—the class that has lost out. On the other hand, we know little or nothing about the attitude of the vast masses who have won out by the revolution, their reactions, their joy, their jubilation.

Viewpoint of the Majority

Having lived with the soldiers in the Red Army, the peasants in the villages, and the workmen in the factories, I feel that I can to some degree present the point of view of this eighty-five per cent of the people.

In discussing the Russian situation, most important of all it is to come to it with some perspective and sense of proportion. Edmund Burke, for example, turned against the French Revolution because, as Buckle says: "His sympathy with present suffering was so intense that he lost all memory of the tyranny by which the sufferings were provoked," I saw some of the sufferings which lay back of the great revolution.

All Had Lost Kinfolk

I drove out one time over those steppe lands about which Gogol exclaims "You steppes, O God, how lovely you are!" There in a little Ukrainian village in a valley the people gathered around the Zemstvo wagon. There were about three hundred women and forty old men and boys and a score of crippled soldiers. The war had stripped the village bare of all able-bodied men. When I stood up to address them I asked: "How many have heard of Washington?" One lad raised his hand. Three had known of Lincoln, ninety knew of Kerensky, and the same number of Lenine. For Tolstoi one hundred and fifty hands went up in the air. They enjoyed this, laughing together at the foreigner and his funny accent. Then came a foolish blunder—I asked: "How many have lost any one in the war?" Nearly every every hand went up before my eyes. And then a cry, a wail, swept through that laughing throng, like a winter wind moaning in the trees. I felt the wagon shaking beneath

my feet.   Two old white bearded peasants
had fallen on the wheels, which shook with
the grief that racked their frames.   A boy
ran out of the crowd, crying: "My brother
—they killed my brother!"   And the wom-
en, three hundred of them, drawing their
platoks to their eyes, or clasped in each
other's arms, wept and wept until I won-
dered where all the tears could come from.
Who could have dreamed that behind those
placid faces lay so much grief and anguish?
Where could one find such concentrated
pain?

No Arms for Soldiers.

And this was but one of the tens of thousands of Russian villages scattered over the
great plains from which all the men marched
away to the war by order of the Czar.   One
of the myriad villages to which came the
wounded, crawling back, crippled, eyeless,
or armless, while millions of others never
returned, for they lie there in that greatest
grave in the world, that grave in Russia
which is 1,500 miles long, extending from
Riga to the Black Sea, which was one time
the Russian front against the Germans.
There Russian peasants with only clubs in

their hands were driven on to fight against
the guns of the Germans, and were mowed
down by the machines. Poor folk of Russia,
what uncounted sacrifices they made of you,
and what unheard of, colossal slaughter!

But where were the guns and ammuni-
tion? They were lying back there in the
snow of Archangel. Cars were very scarce
and profits were high, and bribery of officials was easy. Ten miles out of Archangel
the munitions were dumped in the snow, the
cars were shunted back to be reloaded with
champagne and automobiles and Parisian
dresses, and in Moscow life was gay and
dazzling, and in the trenches life was cold
and bloody and in the little villages life was
dark, fearsome, for millions of hearts were
sore and arms arching for those who lay out
in the snow, massacred as much by the
treachery of the Russians as by the Germans.

The Revolution Starts

All governments exist on the patience and
long suffering of the poor. Though it seems
everlasting there does come an end to it. The
end came in Russia when the masses felt that
more cruel and more vicious and more near

at hand than the Kaiser in Potsdam was their own despotism in Petrograd. But the day of reckoning came. The cup of bitterness for the masses was full. They marched forth against the palaces to end it all. Masses of workingmen poured out from Vibourg raising their cry for bread, land, and peace. When Milukov, looking from his window, saw the throng with the red flag, he said: "There goes the Russian revolution and it will be crushed in fifteen minutes."

But the workingmen came on in spite of the Cossack patrols upon the Nevsky. They came in the face of the drumfire of the machine-guns, they came on until the streets were littered with their bodies. And still they came on, singing and pleading, until the soldiers and Cossacks came over to the people and the Czar and all his retinue were swept away. A shout of joy rang round the world. Strangers kissed each other on the streets. Foreign nations sent to them missions and their congratulations. "Hail to the Revolution of the Russian people."

The people had taken the government away from the Czarists, monarchists, their henchmen and retainers. Now appeared upon the scene the cadets, the lawyers, the professors and the politicians, addressing the people. They, too, offered their congratulations. They said: "People, you have done a noble piece of work. The next task is the formation of a state. It is a hard and difficult task, but we, the educated, intelligent, people, we, who understand this business of governing, are willing to shoulder the responsibility. Noble soldiers you go back to the trenches. Brave workingmen, go back to the machines. And peasants, you go back · to the land."

The Soviets Assemble

Now the Russian people are very tractable and reasonable, and so they went back. But the Russian people are very intelligent, if not literate, with a soil wisdom and a native intelligence, and before they went back they gathered together in little organizations. The munition factories selected one of their members whom they trusted; the men in the cotton factories did likewise; so in the brick yards, the glass works, and all other industries. The different regiments chose a soldier-delegate, sometimes an officer; the teachers' organization selected a teacher; the engineers an engineer. They called this group a Soviet. Delegates were elected, not geographically, but according to trades. Delegates can be removed at any time instead of every two or four years. This was done not only in the big cities, but in the smallest towns and hamlets. It was done in every mine and fishery throughout Russia. Each group sent a delegate to Petrograd. There wasformed the All Russian Soviet of Workmen and Soldiers.

Action Was Spontaneous

There is no more remarkable phenomenon in all history than that after the old state apparatus of the Czar had gone to the scrap heap more than one-sixth of the surface of the world should be dotted over with tens of thousands of these new social organizations. The commander of the battleship "Provost" told me that when the Revolution broke out his ship was in Italian waters. The day after the news came that the Revolution was on, the crew organized itself into a Soviet, which was in all respects like the Soviets of Petrograd, and yet they had no contact with it whatever.

The Soviet then must be regarded as the natural organization of the Russian people. Its roots run back into the older institutions —the **mir** of the village, and the **Artel** of the city.

The Soviet was like an old New England town meeting. Here the people met together and talked as only Russians can talk. The speech suppressed for centuries burst like a flood. "Russia," as Root said, "became a nation of 100,000,000 orators." The Soviet became a clearing house for ideas.

The 150,000,000 peasants of Russia never recognized the right of the great landlords to the land. "The land belongs to God and the people," was always the cry of the peasants. Now, again, the old cry resounded in the forums of the masses. The land belongs to God and the people. So the first demand formulated by the Soviet was "Land to the peasants".

The workingmen likewise threshed out their problems. "We want to be free men," they said. "A free man must have control over his own life. Most of our lives we spend in the factories. Therefore we should have control over the factories." And "Factories to the workers" became the second slogan of the Soviets.

They Wanted Peace

And they talked about peace. Oh yes, it is easy to talk of war when one's stomach is full and the guns and the trenches are far away. But on the Riga front I have seen soldiers gaunt and worn, walking barefoot in the freezing mud. I have seen squads of hungry troops falling upon a field of turnips and devouring them. And to the soldiers in this plight came the ministers from the government saying: "Fight for Russia until we take Constantinople." "Constantinople," cried the soldiers, "We don't want Constantinople, we want peace. We don't want other people to take our land, and neither will we fight to take other people's land." They began to examine those phrases, "War for defense—war for democracy," and they began to doubt. They began to question. "Are our Allies land grabbers and imperialists like Germany and ourselves? More persistently grew the conviction that they had nothing to fight for, and so rolled up the third cry from all over the land: "Peace to the people."

With these three slogans inscribed upon their banners they besieged the Kerensky government, marching by millions in processions, presenting their demands. "Wait awhile," the ministers said; "wait until the end of the war." But as that seemed so far away, and the clamor of the people grew, the ministers said, "Wait until the Constituent Assembly. But month after month that was postponed, and month by month grew the restlessness of the masses, and all the answer to their cries was a change in the ministers and the perpetual "wait, wait, wait".

But after awhile those promises and evasions no longer availed. Their thirst for land and peace was too imperative to be appeased. "If this thing that calls itself a government cannot give the people what they want, let the people take it themselves."

Peasants Seize the Land

In the summer of 1917 the peasants began to seize the land. I remember at this time talking with Baron Nolde. "What is it the peasants want on your estate?" "My estate," he answered. "And how are they going to get it?" I asked. "They got it" was his laconic reply.

In the Tambof government the skies were reddened with the fire from the burning hay ricks and manor houses. Workmen of their own accord began to assume control of the factories. Things happened precisely as one would expect them to happen. The damaging of materials and machinery helped along the general dislocation of industry.

Soldiers, disgusted, began to throw down their guns and march away from the trenches, crowding the cars and contributing to the general breakdown of transportation. Y. M. C. A. men have told me that this happened where soldiers had not even heard the name Bolshevik..

This action roused a rage and furore in the ministers. The "best people", the grandmother and grandfather of the revolution, Breshkovskaya and Tschaikovsky, bade the people be quiet, but they had lost all influence over them. Tserethelli and the "flaming Tscheidize" unloosed their eloquence, but they might as well have shouted at a tidal wave. The government wrote out resolutions, but they might as well have written resolutions to an avalanche. They sent out punitive expeditions to put down the peasants. These troops often went over to the side of the people. The great uprising of the people to possess themselves of land, peace, and the factories, was on—something elemental—a blind striking out which seemed to be plunging Russia over the precipice into chaos and ruin.

Men of Brains Appear

However unfortunate may have been all this upheaval of the people, it was fortunate that there was a party which could recognize facts when it saw them, a party with a set of brains which could see that here was a deep-running, ultra-radical movement, and that for this only an ultra-radical program would suffice. A party which understood the people, and therefore knew how to turn these elemental energies into constructive channels; a party which had the confidence of the people and therefore to whose direction the people would give heed; a party which, I believe, the sober judgment of history will say kept Russia from plunging over the precipice into chaos and night.

It was the party of the Bolsheviks. (Prolonged applause.) It is not quite right to say that the Bolsheviks understood the people or that they had the confidence of the people. This was not necessary. They **were** the people. They were of the rank and file, they spoke the people's language, shared the people's thoughts, the vanguard of thinking workers and peasants. Their stronghold was in those literate sections of the population, like the sailors and Letts. They were mostly young men, not afraid of responsibility, not afraid to die, and—most marvellous of all in Russia, not afraid to work. They were of the working class.

Of course the Bolshevik party had its intelligentzia, Kollonta, Lunacharsky, Bonch-Breuvich, as well as Lenine and Trotzky. They spoke many languages and had written scores of books.

Faith in the People

But they differ from most of the other intelligentzia in this way. The usual intelligentzia want to give the people what they think the people ought to have. The Bolsheviki said: "Let the people decide what they want themselves." The other intelligentzia said: "Let the people rule, but let

them rule through us." The Bolsheviki said,
Let the people rule themselves." They had
a sublime faith in the people. They held
that the emancipation of the working class
can come only from the workers themselves
and not from the schemes hatched up in
somebody's brain and handed to the people.
Delegations of workingmen would come to
Lenine, asking him how to run certain industries and his reply was, "I'm sure I don't
know. You go and run them and then come
back and tell me," adding, humorously, "I
shall write a book about it." (Laughter.)

They had a natural love for the people.
Volodarsky, who was one of the victims of
the Franco-British plot to assassinate the
members of the Soviet, said to me, "I have
had more joy in this year of the revolution
than any fifty men ought to have in all their
lives."

During the tragic summer and fall of
1917, when chaos was growing more cha-
otic, the force and authority of the Kerensky
government was growing weaker day by
day. The Allies were trying manfully to
keep the Kerensky government alive by al-
ternate hypodermic injections of threats and

promises, but in a situation that called for the strength of a giant it was like a babe. Things were growing from bad to worse. The Bolsheviks alone seemed to grasp all the facts and understand that for an ultra-radical movement only an ultra-radical program would suffice. Its program was the program of the people: "Land to the Peasants; Factories to the Workers; Peace to All the World." The Bolsheviks not only accepted the people's program but pointed out the means through which they could carry it into operation. They pointed to the Soviets.

These had now become formidable organizations. The local Soviets had drawn around themselves all the vital revolutionary forces of the community. The vast network of them was being linked up into a well-knit organization.

When the Kerensky government machine was daily growing more discredited and impossible, there had grown up in their very midst this new apparatus. All the Bolsheviki did was to point out this fact and sound the rallying cry: All power to the Soviet." It went like wildfire throughout the land.

"All power to the Soviet." Sailors on the Baltic sent it to their comrades on the fleets in the Black and Yellow and White Seas, and from them it came re-echoing back again.

Bolsheviki Take Government

So when the Bolsheviks raised the cry of "All power to the Soviet," they knew that it meant all power to the people, all power to the revolutionary soldiers and sailors, revolutionary workmen and peasants. A few sailors stepped into the Marinsky palace and told the self-appointed gentlemen with the high-sounding title "Council of the Russian Republic", to go home. Several had apoplectic fits, but they went. (Laughter.) A few hundred soldiers and workmen surrounded the Kerensky Provisional Government in the Winter Palace which was defended by the junkers and Woman's Batallion—total casualties, one junker wounded and one woman fainted.

This transfer of power into the hands of the Soviet from the Atlantic to the Pacific, from the Arctic to the Ukraine, cost less than one life in every thousand of the population, (Prolonged applause.)

Of all the hypocritical pretenses and poses of which this generation is guilty, the most disgraceful and disgusting is the pious posture of horror over the violence of the Russian revolution. This, on the part of nations which have just brought Europe through the most horrible orgy of violence the world has ever known, destroying ten millions of the flower of its youth and almost reducing civilization to a heap of ruins! "But, by these violences," we say, "we overthrew the Kaiser, Prussian militarism, Imperialism, and junkerdom." "And through our violence," the Russian peasants and workers could say, "We overthrew the Russian Czar, Russian imperialism, Russian landlordism and capitalism, and lit the torch of liberty throughout the world." (Prolonged applause.) And who would dare gainsay the greatness of this revolution? Just as we now remember the French revolution and not the Napoleonic wars, it may be that one hundred years from now mankind will glorify the years 1917 and 1918 not for the results that flow from the great war, but for the Russian Revolution. And for every victim of the Russian

Revolution there are one hundred victims of the great war.

Kill Only One in 1,000

Take, if you please, the most exaggerated estimates as to the executions in Moscow and Petrograd, the street fighting in Kiev and Irkutsk, the peasants' outbreaks in the provinces; add up the total and divide it into the population of Russia—not the 3,000,000 involved in the American revolution, nor the 33,000,000 of the French revolution, but the 180,000,000 of the Russian revolution— the result will show a death list of less than one in a thousand of the population.

"But," people exclaim, "the violence of confiscation, ruthless confiscation!" Rightly or wrongly, when the fulfillment of the national destiny of America demanded that we cut the cancer of slavery from our body politic we confiscated the vast property rights, and in doing it we didn't stop until we had killed one in every two hundred of our people. Rightly or wrongly, to fulfill her national destiny, Russia felt it essential to cut out the cancer of Czarism, landlordism and capitalism, from her body politic· This bloodshed was comparatively little, because the masses were so overwhelmingly on one side and because the Slavic spirit finds it so much easier to forgive than to revenge. This restraint is all the more wonderful to those who know the provocation to revenge which comes out of the history of Russia's past.

I need not recall to you the Winter Palace Square where on Bloody Sunday thousands were shot down as they came petitioning the "little father". Remember the tens of thousands sent away to rot in mines and dungeons. Remember the hundreds of thousands of the bravest and best who tracked their way with clanking chains across the snows of Siberia. These statistics are the unemotional symbols of cruelty inflicted by the old order and are not moving. But if you had seen men tottering from the long years they spent in the stone sacks at Schlusselbourg, or if you had seen women with deep scars cut by the **nagaika** of the savage Cossack guards, you might recall the words of Lincoln: "If for every drop of blood drawn by the lash another shall be drawn by the sword, the judgments of the Lord are pure and righteous altogether."

Good for Evil

A most terrific indictment of the old order was in a peasant who stood with clenched fists and teeth before a Soviet placard,, saying, "The old government did not want to tell us anything but to go to work and to go to church and to pay our taxes, but now our Soviet government wants to tell us about the new liberty and freedom, but we cannot read this. The Czar put out our eyes."

When I saw these people rise and take the government in their own hands, and at the same time take the murderers, torturers, and betrayers, in their grasp, I thought there would be the dreaded blood-bath. But then I saw these peasants and workers turn on these men who had lashed them, jailed them, and browbeaten them, not with revenge, but with forgiveness, and as the first act of the new Peasants' and Workmen's government on November 7th, 1917, decreed the abolition of capital punishment. The Soviet, though it had a giant's strength, did not use it as a giant.

Struck in Self-Defense

I haven't the slightest zeal to minimize the violence of the revolution and paint it as a lovely thing. Let it be painted in all its black and bloody colors so that the ruling class will get to work and seek for some other solution of the social question than by the way of repression with its inevitable day of reckoning. But I am speaking now simply from the standpoint of a reporter stating the facts, and the fact is that up to the time of the ending of the civil war, in June, 1918, with the Soviets in complete control over Russia, violence was not the order of the day upon the part of the Workmen's and Peasants' government. When the Allies destroyed the Soviets and, under the protecting wing of its armies, the Black Hundred, Czarists, officers, and landlords returned, loosing upon the peasants and workers, the women and children, the most cruel and savage brutalities, and the counter-revolution raised its ugly head in Moscow and Petrograd, then peasants and workers struck back by the so-called Red Terror of the Soviets.

Cossacks' Machine Guns

But what is the Red Terror of the workingmen and peasants beside the White Terror of their enemies?. Some of these stories have leaked past the censors. Ackerman, of the Times, tells of a train of 2,100 prisoners which left the Urals and six weeks later arrived at Nikolsk with 1,300. "What became of the other 800?" he asks. The train was without sanitation or provisions, and these 800 were starved to death, committed suicide or were shot in trying to escape from their hell. Many died in the arms of the Red Cross workers in Nikolsk. That was only one of several such trains of misery and death, he adds. The same reporter tells of the Cossack, Kalmikoff, whom the Allies sent before them on the Trans-Siberian, burning villages and terrorizing the people so that they did not dare to pick up the corpses of the slain but left them lying on the streets to be eaten by the dogs.

When this brutal bandit, the protege of democracy, entered Habarovsk he was so angered to find the Soviet Commissars had escaped that he took sixteen innocent people, whose chief crime was that they were teach-

ers of the children of workmen and peasants,
lined them up against a wall and mowed
them down with machine guns, their blood
crimsoning the flower beds they had taught
the children to make.

But why repeât these brutalities of the
class war?   Some day both sides will be
brought together before the bar of history.
On one side will be the peasants and workers charged with the Red Terror of the Revolution. On the other side will be ranged the
monarchists, officers, and the landloards,
charged with the White Terror of the counter-revolution.   When they raise their hands
for judgment, the gnarled and calloused and
toilworn hands of the workingmen and peasants will be white as compared with the
crimson stains of the gentlemen and ladies
of privilege.   (Prolonged applause.)

But why should we look at the furies and
sounds of the revolution, and not at the revolution itself?   Why hold to our provincial
viewpoint and with a yardstick try to meas-
ure this upheaval of the human spirit—the
greatest since the Crusaders?

Why not see the wonder and glory of
150,000,000 people breaking their chains

and emerging from the night of feudalism, blinded at first but acting toward their oppressors without vengeance, patiently waiting their leaders to give them the desires of their hearts—land, peace, and factories— then as they grew ever more clear in their purpose and conscious of their powers, we see them with a giant's strength reach out and take their state within their grasp. (Prolonged applause.)

Demobilize Vast Army

With the first task that fell upon the newly organized Soviet Americans ought to have a deal of sympathy. We are staggered by the problem of demobilizing 4,000,000 soldiers yet the new aparatus of the Soviets had suddenly thrown upon it 12,000,000 troops and there was nothing more serious than the shooting up of a few railway stations. Some one interjects "They didn't demobilize these soldiers—the soldiers demobilized themselves." That is precisely the point. The Soviet is a new organization that brings automatically into action new integrating forces of humanity, forces that were latent but unutilized. While the Soviet was look-

public instruction is the honor and glory of every people." This is a noble statement, but how does it work out in practice? In the Far East Soviet, at Habarovsk, was the motto "Detye nadezhde meera."——"Children the hope of the world." Way back in Siberia these young teachers never heard of the Montessori method, but out of their own consciousness they evolved a system which is the equivalent of it.

An old peasant one day appeared in the Childrens'. School. "Children, these hands cannot write," he said, holding them up, toilworn and calloused, "they cannot write because the only thing the Czar wanted them for was to plough." As the tears coursed down his cheeks he said, "but you, the children of a new Russia, you can learn to write. Oh, that I might begin again as a child in the New Russia!"

What Gorky Said

Maxim Gorky says: "The cultural creative work of the Russian Soviet government which is going on under the most difficult conditions and which requires heroic exertions, is now about to have a scope and a form which have hitherto been unknown in the history of mankind. This is no exaggeration. A short time ago I was still an opponent of our Bolshevik government and am still in many ways in disagreement with its methods of work, but I still know that the historians of the future, when they come to estimate the value of the work that has been done by the Russian workers in the course of a year, will be unable to avoid admiring the magnificence of their creative work in the realm of culture."

The struggle of the Red Army is shown best in its victories upon fifteen fronts.

It is apparent that you can't have a great growing army and a great growing cultural life without something back of them. So these two facts effectually dispose of the stories of mere chaos, anarchy, in Russia.

Increased Production

So when we turn to the third realm of Soviet activity, economic reorganization, we can see in the decrees the blue prints of reconstruction for the new economic life upon a co-operative basis. It is one thing to write out magnificent plans on paper. It is quite another matter to translate them into actual life. At the great capitals one would see mostly confusion, but in the provinces even last June, workmen's control was sloughing off its fantastic and impossibilist features and gradually attaining discipline and an actual increase of output.

As soon as the workmen found the factories really in their own hands there came a change in their minds. Under the Kerensky regime they had tended to elect a foreman for his leniency. Under their own government, the Soviet, they began to elect as foremen those who put discipline into the shop and raised the production.

The first time I met Krasnoschekoff, the head of the Far East Soviet, he was talking pessimistically about the industrial outlook. "For every word I say to the bourgeoisie against their sabotaging I say ten words to the workmen against their slackness. But I believe the change is coming." When I saw him the last of June he was in a happy, jubilant mood. The change had come, and in the six factories he said that they were producing more than ever before.

A New Kind of Music

In the so-called "American works", the wheels, frames and brakes of cars, shipped from the United States, were assembled and the cars sent out over the Trans-Siberian Railway. Under the Kerensky regime these shops had been hotbeds of trouble, one disturbance following close upon the heels of another. The 6,000 workmen on the pay roll were turning out but 18 cars a day. The Soviet committee closed the plant down and then completely reorganized the shops, reducing the force to 1,800 men. In the underframe section, instead of 1,400 there were now 350; but by means of short cuts introduced by the workers themselves, the output of that department was increased. Altogether, the 1,800 men on the new pay roll were turning out 12 cars a day—an efficiency increase of more than 100 per cent per man.

One day I was standing with Soochanov on the hills overlooking the shops. He was listening to the clank of the cranes and the stamp of the trip hammers rising up from the valley.

"That seems to be sweet music in your ears," I said.

"Yes," he replied, "the old revolutionists used to make a noise with bombs, but this is the noise of the revolutionists hammering out the new social order." (Laughter and applause.)

Under the Kerensky regime the workmen were asking for ever higher and higher wages. The Soviet put a stop to that at once. It worked upon the principle that the pay of officials. of a workingman's government should not be more than that of an average workman. No one can have cake until every one has bread. They fixed the pay at $60, with $10 extra for each non-earning member of the family. Lenine's wife works in the Department of Education, therefore Lenine receives only $60 a month. Trotzky has a wife and two children, therefore he receives $90 a month. Whenever, then, any workman gets the itch for a fatter pay envelope his fellows ask him: "So, you want a larger salary than Lenine or Trotzky?"

When the Soviet government moved to Moscow it took over one of the large hotels, the National, to live in. The first thing it did was to abolish expensive and elaborate menus. The meals, instead of consisting of many dishes, were cut down to two courses. One could have soup and meat, or soup and kasha (a kind of porridge). Of course there was tea.

Helped End the War

To the people the Revolution was a good thing. Naturally they wanted to pass it along, so through the Soviet they concentrated their efforts upon the creation of a revolution in Germany. To this end the Russian Soviet published millions of copies of papers in different languages, German, Hungarian, Czech, etc. These papers were dropped by aeroplanes, blown by wind, smuggled in boxes, and carried by the prisoners into Germany.

Our military experts were saying that the war would last six months or two years more, and that it might take a million American lives in order to reach the Rhine. Yet while the Teuton armies were way down upon the soil of France and Italy they suddenly stopped fighting. Why? Because suddenly the revolution started back home, the German Imperial government collapsed, and Peace came.

Now in this happy event the hammering of the Allied guns on the western front played their part, hunger played its part, but so did the Soviet government play its great part. As Douglas Young, the British Consul at Archangel, says: "Bolshevik propaganda had as much to do with the sudden collapse of Germany as our military operations." While we are working up our frenzy against the Bolsheviks let us not forget what they did toward saving a million of American soldiers' lives.

Value of the Soviets

In these economic and military ways, in cultural realms, and in the moral prestige of political victory the Soviet is growing stronger day by day. I remember a session of the Vladivostok Soviet when one of the Right was making a furious attack upon the Soviet at a time when the food rations had been cut down. "The Bolsheviks promised you lots of things," he said, "but they didn't give them to you, did they? They promised you bread, but where is it? Where is the bread that———" The words of the speaker were drowned in a storm of whistles and hisses.

It is true that the Soviet did not give these material things, but man does not live by bread alone and neither do the Soviets live merely by the bread alone that they can feed the people. They live by grace of other values which they offer. The Soviets hold the loyalty and affection of the people, not by the satisfaction of the hunger of the stomach but by the satisfaction of the hunger of the heart and the mind.

Conscripts of a Dream

All men crave fellowship. The Soviet offers a place where they can work together almost as a family because they understand and grasp what they are doing. Even the lowest man here feels his human worth. All men crave power. Through this institution, which, as the common people, they have themselves operated, they have tasted power, and the workingman is like any other human being. He is loath to let that power go. All men crave adventure. The Soviet offers men the greatest adventure in all the world

—creating a new justice, a new order of economics, a new order of society. All men have a spiritual passion. It needs only to be aroused. The Soviet has aroused the dull, complacent, plodding peasant, so that he is the conscript of a mighty dream—a dream expressed best in these words of Gorky:

"At different periods nearly every people has felt itself to be the Messiah who was called to save the world and that in itself is born the best and most ideal force. . . . And it is now plain that on the Russian people, starving, tortured by three centuries of slavery, worn out by the war, history has now laid its great mission, while under the threat of being crushed by robbers. . . . In the midst of all this Russia says to the workers and to the right-minded people of the whole world: 'Come and go with us toward the new life, whose creation we work for without sparing ourselves and without sparing anybody or anything. Erring and suffering in the great joy of labor and in the burning hope of progress, we leave to the honest judgment of history all our deeds. Come with us to the battle against the ancient order to work for a new form of life. Forth to life's freedom and beauty!'"

The verdict of the Russian worker upon the Soviet is that it has made good. Toward the mistakes and failings of the Soviet his attitude is the same as toward his individual mistakes—a very lenient one. He knows that the Soviet has not brought the millenium. On the contrary, he understands that conditions are very bad. But the Russian understands fully the terrible handicaps the Soviet had to face.

When the Soviet took over the government they had as their heritage the wreckage of 300 years of autocracy, a three years' war, and a state-shattering revolution. They were at first deserted by the intelligentzia, excommunicated by the church, sabotaged by the old officials, nearly guillotined by the Germans, blockaded and boycotted by the Allies. That the Soviet, beset and bedeviled on all sides should have survived at all is wonderful. That it should actually have forged ahead is the best tribute to its basic strength.

The Red Funeral in Vladivostok

THE RED FUNERAL IN VLADIVOSTOK

It was the Fourth of July. I was standing on the Kitaiskaya looking down upon the holiday flags on the American battleship in Vladivostok Bay. Suddenly I heard a far away sound. 'Listening, I caught the strains of the Revolutionary Hymn:—
With hearts heavy and sad we bring our dead
Who shed their blood in the fight for fredom.

Looking up, I saw on the crest of the hill the first lines of the funeral procession of the gruzshchiki.

Four days before, when the Czecho-Slo-vaks, aided by Japanese and English troops, suddenly seized the Soviet and its officials, throwing confusion and terror into the ranks of the workers, the gruzshchiki (longshoremen), rushed into the Red Staff Building, and, though outnumbered forty to one, refused to surrender until the building was fired by an incendiary bomb.

Today, the people were burying the defenders of the fallen Soviet. Out of the workmen's quarters they streamed, jamming the street, not from curb to curb, but from wall to wall. They came billowïng over the hilltop by thousands until the whole long slope was choked with the dense, slow-moving throng, keeping time to the funeral march of the revolutionists.

Up through the gray and black mass of men and women ran two lines of white-bloused sailors of the Bolshevik fleet. Above their heads tossed a cloud of crimson standards with silvered cords and tassels. In the vanguard, four men carried a huge red banner with the words: "Long Live the Soviet of Workmen's and Peasants' Deputies! Hail to the International Brotherhood of the Toilers!"

A hundred girls in white, carrying the green wreaths from forty-four unions of the city, formed a guard of honor for the coffins of the gruzshchiki, which, with the red paint still wet upon them, were borne upon the shoulders of their comrades. The music crashed out by the Red Fleet Band was lost in the volume of song that rose from the seventeen thousand singers.

Here was color and sound and motion— but there was something else, a something

which compelled fear and awe. I have seen
a score of the great processions of Petrograd
and Moscow, peace and victory and protest
and memorial parades, military and civilian.
They were all vast and impressive because
the Russians have a genius for this kind of
thing. But this was different.

From these defenseless poor, stropped of
their arms, and with sorrowing songs bear-
ing off their dead, there came a threat more
menacing than that which frowned from the
twelve-inch guns of the Allied Fleet, riding
in the harbor below. It was impossible not
to feel it. It was so simple, so spontaneous
and so elemental. It came straight out of
the heart of the people. It was the people,
leaderless, isolated, beaten to earth, thrown
upon its own resources, and yet, out of its
.grief, rising magnificently to take command
of itself.

The dissolution of the Soviet, instead of
plunging the people into inactive grief and
dissipating their forces, begot a strange, uni-
fying spirit. Seventeen thousand separate
souls were welded into one. Seventeen thousand people, singing in unison found themselves thinking in unison. With a common

mass will and mass consciousness, they formulated their decisions from their class standpoint—the determined standpoint of the revolutionary proletariat.

The Czecho Slovaks came, offering a guard of honor. "Ne noozhna!" (It is not necessary!" the people replied. "You killed our comrades. Forty to one you fought against them. They died for the Soviet and we are proud of them. We thank you, but we cannot let the guns which shot them down guard them in their death!"

"But there may be danger for you in this city," said the authorities.

"Never mind," they answered, "We, too, are not afraid of death. And what better way to die than beside the bodies of our comrades!"

Some bourgeois societies came, presenting memorial wreaths. (The Cadets officially denied that these wreaths came from them.)

"Ne noozhna, it is not necessary," the people answered. "Our comrades died in a struggle against the bourgeoisie. They died fighting cleanly. We must keep their memory clean. We thank you, but we dare not lay your wreaths upon their coffins."

The procession poured down the Aleutskaiya Hill, filled the large, open space at the bottom, and faced up toward the English Consulate. Near by was a workcar with a tower for repairing electric wires. Whether it was there by design or accident I do not know. Presently it was to serve as a speaker's rostrum.

The band played a solemn dirge. The men bared their heads. The women bowed. The music ceased and there was a silence. The band played a second time. Again there was the bowing and baring of heads and again the long silence. And yet there was no speaker. It was like a huge Quaker meeting in the open air. And just as a sermon has no place in Russian public worship so here a speech was not essential to this act of public devotion. But should some one from the people feel the impulse to speak there was the platform awaiting him. It was as if in the pause the people were generating a voice.

At last out of the crowd one came and climbed upon the high platform. He had not the gift of oratory but his frequent iteration, "They died for us," "They died for us," touched others to utterance.

Most eloquent of all was a lad of seventeen, the secretary of a league of young Socialists. "We were students and artists and such kind of people. We held ourselves aloof from the Soviet," he said. "It seemed to us foolish for workmen to govern without the wisdom of the wise. But now we know that you were right and we were wrong. From now on we shall stand with you. What you do we will do. We pledge our tongues and pens to make known the wrongs that you have suffered the length and breadth of Russia and throughout the world."

Suddenly the word went through the throng that Constantin Soochanov had been paroled until five o'clock and that he was coming with counsels of peace and moderation. Soochanov was the president of the Soviet, a student twenty-four years of age, son of a high official of the Tsar, and a hero in a revolution that is not given to hero-worship.

While some were affirming his coming and others were denying it, he himself appeared. He was quickly passed along upon the shoulders of the sailors. In a storm of cheers, he climbed the ladder and came out upon the platform-top, smiling. . . .

As if to avert the flood of tragedy and pathos that beat suddenly upon him from every side, he turned his head away. His eyes fell for the first time upon the red coffins of the men who had been slain in defense of his Soviet and upon the mothers, wives and children of the men who lay within them. That was too much for him. A shudder passed through his frame, he threw up his hands, staggered, and would have fallen headlong into the crowd, but a friend caught him. With both hands pressed to his face, Soochanov, in the arms of his comrades, sobbed like a child. We could see his breath come and go and the tears raining down his cheeks. The Russians are little given to tears. But that day there were seventeen thousand Russians who sobbed with their young leader on the public square of Vladivostok.

But Soochanov knew that many tears were an indulgence and that he had a big and serious task to perform. Fifty feet behind him was the English Consulate and fifty rods before him were the waters of the Golden Horn with the frowning guns of the Allied Fleet.   He wrenched himself away from his grief and   .   .   .   with an ever mounting passion of earnestness he spoke, closing with the words which shall henceforth be the rallying cry for the workers in Vladivostok and the Far East:—

"Here, before the Red Staff Building where our comrades gruzsachiki were slain, we swear by these red coffins that hold them, by their wives and children that weep for them, by the red banners which float over them, that the Soviet for which they died shall be the thing for which we live—or if need be—like them, die.   Henceforth the return of the Soviet shall be the goal of all our sacrifice and devotion.   To that end we shall fight with every means.   The bayonets have been wrested from our hands, but when the day comes and we have no guns we shall fight with sticks and clubs, and when these are gone then with our bare fists and bodies. Now it is for us to fight only with our minds and spirits.   Let us make them hard and strong and unyielding.   The Soviet is dead. Long live the Soviet!"

The crowd caught up the closing words in a tremendous demonstration, mingled with the strains of the "International":—

"Arise ye prisoners of starvation
Arise ye wretched of the earth,
For Justice thunders condemnation
A better world's in birth——"

The resolution proclaiming the restoration of the Soviet, the objective of all the future struggles of the revolutionary proletariat and peasants of the Far East, was read. At the call for the vote seventeen thousand hands shot into the air. They were the hands which had built the cars and paved the streets, forged the iron, held the plough, and swung the hammer. All kinds of hands they were: the big, rough hand of the old gruzsachiki, the artisans' deft and sinewy, the knotted hands of the peasants, thick with callouses, and thousands of the frailer, whiter hands of the working women. But these hands the riches of the Far East had been wrought. They were no different from the nscarred, stained hands of labor anywhere in all the world. Except in this regard. For a time they had held the power. The Government had been within their grasp. Four days ago it had been wrested from their grasp but the feel of it was still within their hands—these hands raised now in solemn pledge to take that power again. . . .

A sailor striding down from the hilltop, pushed through the crowd and climbed upon the platform, "Comrades!" he cried joyously. "We are not alone. I ask you to look away to the flags flying over there on the American battleship. You cannot see them down there where you stand. But they are there. And with the flags of all the other nations there is the red flag of our Russian Republic. No, comrades, we are not alone today in our grief. The Americans understand and they are with us!"

It was a mistake of course. Those flags had been hung out in celebration of our Day of Independence. But the crowd did not know that. To them it was like the sudden touch of a friend's hand upon a lonely traveler in a foreign land. With enthusiasm they caught up the cry of the sailor: "The Americans are with us!" And the vast conclave, lifting up their coffins, wreaths and banners were once more in motion. They were go-

ing to the cemetery but not directly. Tired
as they were from long standing in the sun,
they made a wide detour to reach the street
that runs up the steep hill to the American
Consulate. Then straight up the sharp slope
they toiled in a cloud of dust, still singing as
they marched, until they came before the
Stars and Stripes floating from the flagstaff.
And there they stopped and laid the coffins
of their dead beneath the flag of the great
Western democracy.

They stretched out their hands, crying,
"Speak to us a word!" They sent delegates
within to implore that word. On the day the
great Republic of the West celebrated its independence the poor and disinherited of
Russia came asking sympathy and understanding in the struggle for their independence. Afterward, I heard a Bolshevik leader
bitterly resentful at this "compromise with
revolutionary honor and integrity."

"How stupid of them," he said. "How
inane of them! Have we not told them that
all countries are alike—all imperialists? Was
this not repeated to them over and over
again by their leaders?"

Truly it had been. But with this demonstration of the Fourth of July the leaders had little to do. They were in prison. The affair was in the hands of the people themselves. And, however cynical many leaders were about the professions of America, the people were not so. In the hour of their affliction, these simple trusting folk, makers of the new democracy of the East, came stretching forth their hands to the great, strong democracy of the West.

They knew that President Wilson had given his assurance of help and loyalty to the "people of Russia." They reasoned: "We the workers and peasants, the vast majority here in Vladivostok, are we not the people? Today in our trouble we come to claim the promised help. Our enemies have taken away our Soviet. They have killed our comrades. We are alone and in distress and you alone of all the nations of the earth can understand." No finer tribute could they offer than to come thus, bringing their dead, with the faith that out of America would come compassion and understanding. America, their only friend and refuge.

But America did not understand.. The American people did not even hear a word about it. But these Russian folk did not know that the American people never heard about it. All they know is that a few weeks after that appeal came the landing of the American troops.

And now they say to one another: "How stupid we were to stand there in the heat and the dust stretching out our hands like beggars!"

*　　*　　*　　*　　*

There was an election in Vladivostok on the last Sunday in July, while the city was under complete control of the Allied forces. The Soviet leaders were in jail and their papers properly suppressed. There were sixteen tickets in the field but, to make a gesture of fairness, the Bolsheviks were allowed ticket number 17. It was taken for granted that few would dare or care to vote for it. There was a great surprise for all the Allies when the ballots were counted up. It was found that the Bolshevik ticket had received more votes than all the other sixteen parties combined. Whereupon the elections were quashed.

But though they have temporarily crushed the Soviet, they have not subdued the spirit of the men that made the Soviet. They have only put steel in their souls and iron in their blood. In their prison on the top of the hill they were always singing. Some one had taught them the words of the English Transport Workers' song, and as I was leaving them, out from their prison, over the Allied battleships lying in the harbor, across the blue waters of the Pacific, there rang out this message to the workers of America:—

"Hold the fort, for we are coming,
Union men be strong;
Side by side we battle onward;
Victory will come."

STUDY SOCIALISM

The great war has made the old competitive system no longer possible. Each warring nation is taking over an increasing share of production, and the question now is whether the nation shall be controlled by the workers or by the bondholders. We Socialists think it should be controlled by the workers. Read these books and you will agree with us.

Shop Talks on Economics. By Mary Marcy. Explains why the wage-workers create wealth and then turn most of it over to the capitalists. Clear, simple, forcible, just the book to start with. Price 10 cents.

Industrial Socialism. By William D. Haywood and Frank Bohn. Explains the ways in which the workers are organizing in the shops and on the political field, to take the control of industry from the capitalists. Price 10 cents.

Socialism Made Easy. By James Connolly. A straight-from-the-shoulder book of Socialist argument by a comrade who was executed after the uprising at Dublin. Price 10 cents.

Value, Price and Profit. By Karl Marx. A brief and scientific explanation of the process by which the employer buys the workers' labor-power, and sells it at a profit. Price 15 cents.

Socialism, Utopian and Scientific. By Frederick Engels. A great book written nearly fifty years ago and predicting the social changes now in progress, explaining their causes and the outcome. Price 15 cents.

The Question Box. By Frank M. Eastwood. Straightforward answers to the many questions about Socialism that are constantly asked by inquirers and critics. Price 10 cents.

The Communist Manifesto. By Marx and Engels. First published in 1847, this wonderful document has been translated into all European languages, and is still the text-book of the coming revolution. Price 10 cents.

Evolution and Revolution. By Mark Fisher. This is a brief industrial history of the human race from primitive times to the present, showing how changes in methods of production bring new classes into power. Price 10 cents.

The Right to Be Lazy. By Paul Lafargue. A brilliant satire pointing out the fact that what the workers need is not more work but more of the good things their work creates. Price 10 cents.

Scientific Socialism Study Course. Prepared especially for study clubs and classes. Questions and answers, the latter mostly taken from the Socialist classics. Price 10 cents.

Any of these books mailed on receipt of price.

CHARLES H. KERR & COMPANY, Publishers

341 East Ohio Street, Chicago

CAPITAL

A Critique of Political Economy

By KARL MARX

This work is beyond comparison the greatest of all Socialist books. It is a scientific analysis of the society in which we live, showing the precise method by which the capitalists grow rich at the expense of the wage-workers.

VOLUME I, entitled **"The Process of Capitalist Production,"** is practically complete in itself. It explains the thing which, up to the time that Marx came on the scene, had confused all the economists, namely, **Surplus Value.** It explains exactly how the capitalist extracts his profits. This volume might be called the keystone of the Socialist arch. 869 pages, **$2.00.**

VOLUME II, **"The Process of Circulation of Capital,"** explains the part that the merchant and the banker play in the present system, and the laws that govern social capital. Unravels knots in which previous writers had become entangled. 618 pages, **$2.00.**

VOLUME III, in some respects the most interesting of all, treats of **"The Process of Capitalist Production as a Whole."** Predicts the **rise of Trusts** and makes clear the **cause of panics and industrial crises.** Shows how the small capitalist is swallowed. Explains for all time the subjects of **Land, Rent and Farming.** 1,048 pages, $2.00.

The complete work sells for $6.00, and contains over 2,500 large pages, in three handsome volumes, bound in cloth and stamped in gold. Any capitalist publishing house would charge at least double our price. Ours is a socialist co-operative house, owned by three thousand comrades who expect no dividends but have subscribed for shares to make possible the circulation of the best socialist literature at the lowest possible prices. Ask for catalog.

CHARLES H. KERR & COMPANY

341 East Ohio Street, Chicago

The Ancient Low

A History of the Ancient Working People from the]
Times to the Adoption of Christianity by Consl
By C. Osborne Ward. Cloth, two volumes, 690 a)
pages. Each, $2.00. Either volume sold separate]

Before written history began, society was already (
into exploiting and exploited classes, master and slav
and subject, ruler and ruled. And from the first the
class has written the histories, written them in acco
with its own interests and from its own point of view.

To arrive at the real story of the life of the op]
classes in ancient times was a task of almost incredib]
culties. To this work Osborne Ward gave a lifetime
gent research, and his discoveries are embodied in tl
volumes entitled The Ancient Lowly. He has gathei
gether into a connected narrative practically everythir
taining to his subject in the published literature of Gree
Rome, including in his inquiry many rare works only
consulted in the great European libraries. But he did n
here. Many of the most important records of the ;
labor unions are preserved only in the form of stone
that have withstood the destructive forces of the cei
and the author traveled on foot many hundreds of miles ;
the Mediterranean Sea, deciphering these inscriptions.

Perhaps the most startling of his conclusions
Christianity was originally a movement of organized
The persecution of the early Christians is shown to have
from the age-long class struggle between exploiters a
ploited. And the most dangerous thing about the boo
the capitalist view-point is that the author does not
make assertions; he proves them.

CHARLES H. KERR & COMPAN

341 E. Ohio Street, Chicago

Check Out More Titles From HardPress Classics Series In this collection we are offering thousands of classic and hard to find books. This series spans a vast array of subjects – so you are bound to find something of interest to enjoy reading and learning about.

Subjects:
Architecture
Art
Biography & Autobiography
Body, Mind &Spirit
Children & Young Adult
Dramas
Education
Fiction
History
Language Arts & Disciplines
Law
Literary Collections
Music
Poetry
Psychology
Science
…and many more.

Visit us at www.hardpress.net

SD - #0119 - 041124 - C0 - 229/152/4 - PB - 9780371792339 - Gloss Lamination